Free Ideas For Video Game Things
Adam Jeremy Capps

Free Ideas For Video Game Things
2022, Adam Jeremy Capps
Public Domain

"It's A Secret To Everybody"

A new public domain book.

Controller Designs part 5

 Action buttons that light up with different colors

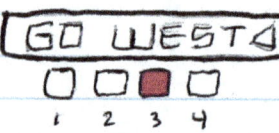 Text display on controller

GO WEST◁ Cycle through
1 2 3 4 4 messages (here red is a priority.)

How color light buttons can be used in a game: red = no, green = yes. Red = block, green = go. Green = buy, yellow = sale. You can go to any thing of a color. Press blue to go toward an ocean. Fire = red, blue = water, yellow = air, green = earth, while casting spells. Flashing red = a warning, danger ahead. Flashing green = "you are near." And a dice kind of thing such as a random group of colors appearing meaning a certain thing.

—Adam Capps

Controller designs part 6

Some random components to consider

1.) A dial to increase or decrease things.
To raise power or lower it. To spend
more or less energy. To buy more
or less things. To zoom in or out
and other things. The dial can
be rotary, sliding, or lever based.
I would suggest one right after
the R button, if a slide., if a
lever then by the thumb. If rotary
around the middle of the controller.

2.) A toggle switch for changing about
3 options "low to high," switching
speed of a thing perhaps. Even
changing the environment such
as "after you are able to enter
into the dark world," you flip
between one and the other.

3) An identation below the L
& R buttons w/ an extra button
tucked in.

4.) One of the action
buttons slide to make
a fifth button, as
shown here: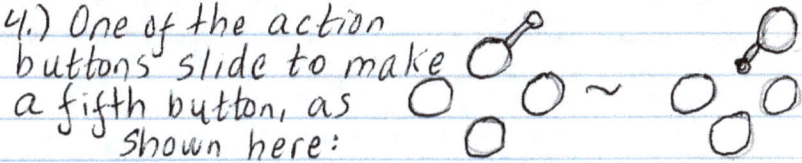

Design 1 w/ Variations.

+ "Slimy X"

Adam Jeremy Capps

controller concept

Some games may come w/ one peripheral.
such as a gun controller. This game
would come w/ more.

For example:

 a laser gun

 a small keyboard-control
the game w/ musical aspects.

 a watch w/a special
display

Gamers may appreciate a game
more if it comes w/ so much.

Adam Jeremy Capps

Console designs List 2

A.

B.

C.

D.

E.

F.

Game controller designs
List 1 : *unique button design*

rotates?

G.C. Designs List 2

more unique button placements

G.C. Designs: List 3

for action buttons & D pad

Buttons on top of a D-pad

OR

extra rectangular buttons

key-board like

"Circular" D-pad

("O" Pad)

Adam J. Cappa

G.C. Designs List 4

a.

B.

C.

D.

E.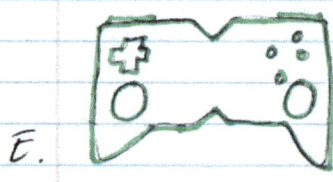

F.

G.

H.

Adam Capps

Console designs List 3
general shape ideas

A.

B.

C.

D.

E.

F.

G.

H.

J.

I.

Controller Designs part 5

 Action buttons that light up with different colors

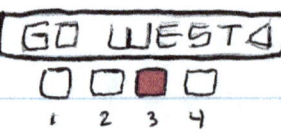 Text display on controller

Cycle through 4 messages (here red is a priority.)

How color light buttons can be used in a game: red = no, green = yes. Red = block, green = go. Green = buy, yellow = sale. You can go to any thing of a color. Press blue to go toward an ocean. Fire = red, blue = water, yellow = air, green = earth, while casting spells. Flashing red = a warning, danger ahead. Flashing green = "you are near." And a dice kind of thing such as a random group of colors appearing meaning a certain thing.

—Adam Capps

Controller designs part 6

Some random components to consider

1.) A dial to increase or decrease things.
To raise power or lower it. To spend
more or less energy. To buy more
or less things. To zoom in or out
and other things. The dial can
be rotary, sliding, or lever based.
cl would suggest one right after
the R button, if a slide., if a
lever then by the thumb. elf rotary
around the middle of the controller.

2.) A toggle switch for changing about
3 options "low to high," switching
speed of a thing perhaps. Even
changing the environment such
as "after you are able to enter
into the dark world," you flip
between one and the other.

3) An identation below the L
& R buttons w/ an extra button
tucked in.

4.) One of the action
buttons slide to make
a fifth button, as
   shown here:

Controller designs part 7

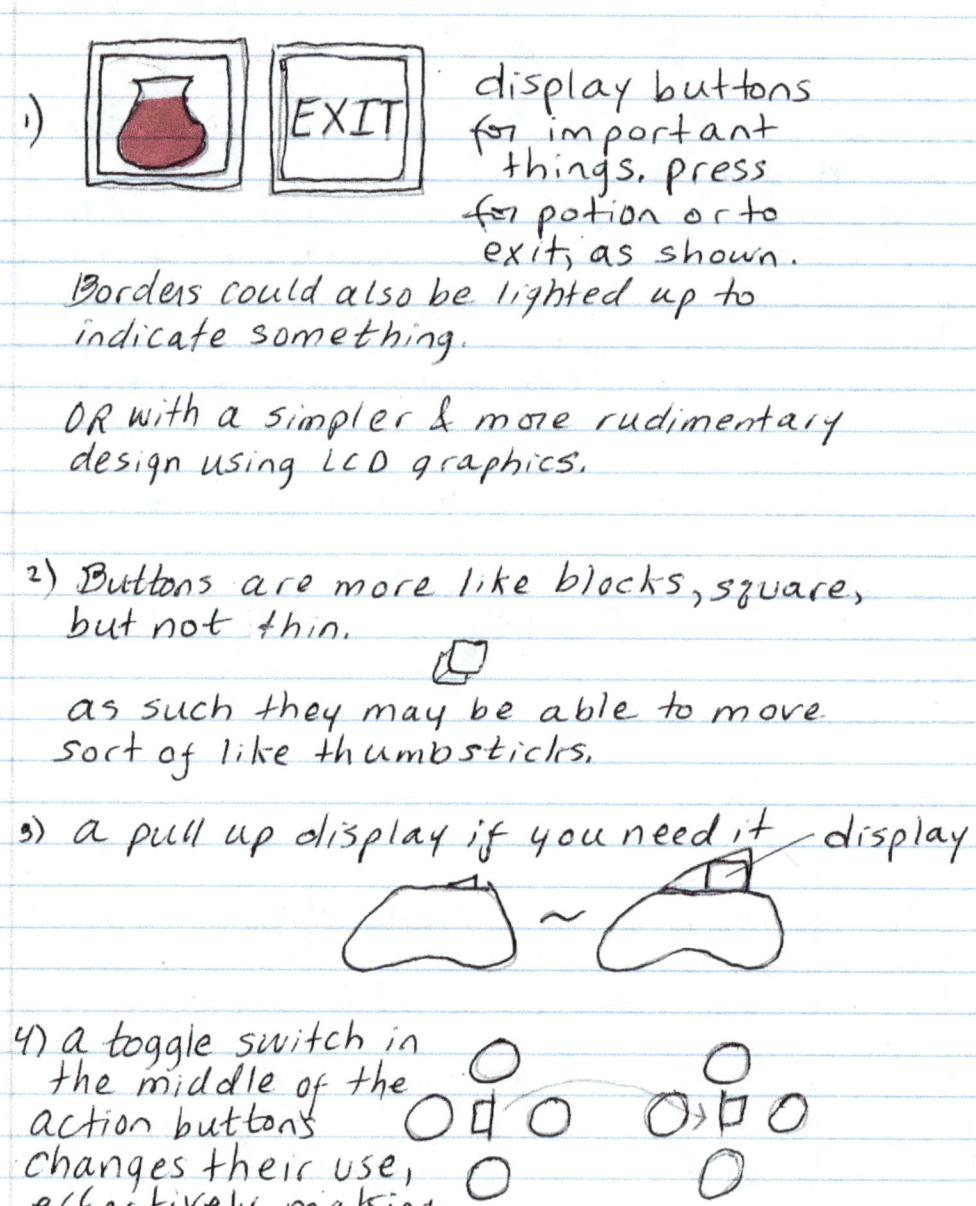

1) display buttons for important things. press for potion or to exit, as shown. Borders could also be lighted up to indicate something.

OR with a simpler & more rudimentary design using LCD graphics.

2) Buttons are more like blocks, square, but not thin.

as such they may be able to move sort of like thumbsticks.

3) a pull up display if you need it ⟶ display

4) a toggle switch in the middle of the action buttons changes their use, effectively making four extra buttons.

—Adam Capps

console designs part 4

Consoles that look like other things

1.)
Looks like bones

2.) Looks like a skull (might make it more menacing than this)

3.) Looks like a big shining diamond. maybe some appealing gems as well.

4.) Cat Like

5.) Bat Like 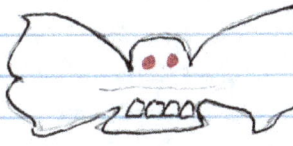 or butterfly?

6.) Row of skulls for controller inputs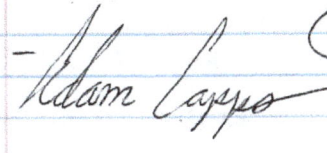

— Adam Caspe

some random ideas

1.) An encyclopedic RPG. Its content & substance comes from that encyclopedia. B= Battle, S=store, V= village (or P= places) S= spells, all in a more D&D style of game.

2.) LCD game w/ gimmiks, as they need them. In other words, LCD games as are lack substance. And for example Nintendo added a second screen.

3.) Random music change. Every now and then a different melody sneaks in, randomly.

4.) Speed gaming mode. An option for players to set conditions & things for them.

5.) Randomizer mode. people create them for games all the time, the original game maker should too. Such a thing could be a reward for beating the game.

6.) A new power glove (for the NES?) now that technology has caught up to its potential.

— Adam Capps

Games that would benefit
From a mod

1.) Drakkhen (SNES) Imagine it w/
the FX chip — helping its 3D intents

2.) Dr. Jekyll & Mr. Hyde (NES)

3.) Willow (NES) said to be a bit bland
graphically in certain places.

4.) Bill & Ted's Excellent Adventure (NES)
You might even mod it into "Bill
and Ted's Bogus Journey"!

5.) So many LJN NES games. Many
of them have a good basis, but
poorly executed.

6.) A game that makes Adventure
Island a game more mario-esque.

7.) Any time a game could use better
graphics is almost always, even
if something was good enough
graphically to begin with. Such
was done w/ Street Fighter 2,
the Genesis version. & especially
when a game had a good basis/
concept, but was poorly designed
otherwise.
                        —Adam Capps

making video game based

Videos, such as for YouTube, the different kinds:

1) Buying - at a store, a conventions, live, or as "pick up" videos.
2) Come in mail videos if you have people mailing you things
3) Top Tens, worst of, best of.
4) Evolution of
5) The first of every level, the hardest level per, and things like that
6.) History of the game, the console, ect.
7.) Simple reviews
8.) Hidden gems
9.) Best graphics per system (games with the best graphics on any given console.)
10.) Speed runs
11.) Most valuable
12) Rarest
13.) playthrough/walkthrough
14.) Comparisons - like comparing the graphics of the same game on another system
15.) During Halloween make a spooky games kind of video
16.) magazine reading/showing like w/ EGM or Nintendo power.
17) Competitions

- Adam Capps

console designs part 5

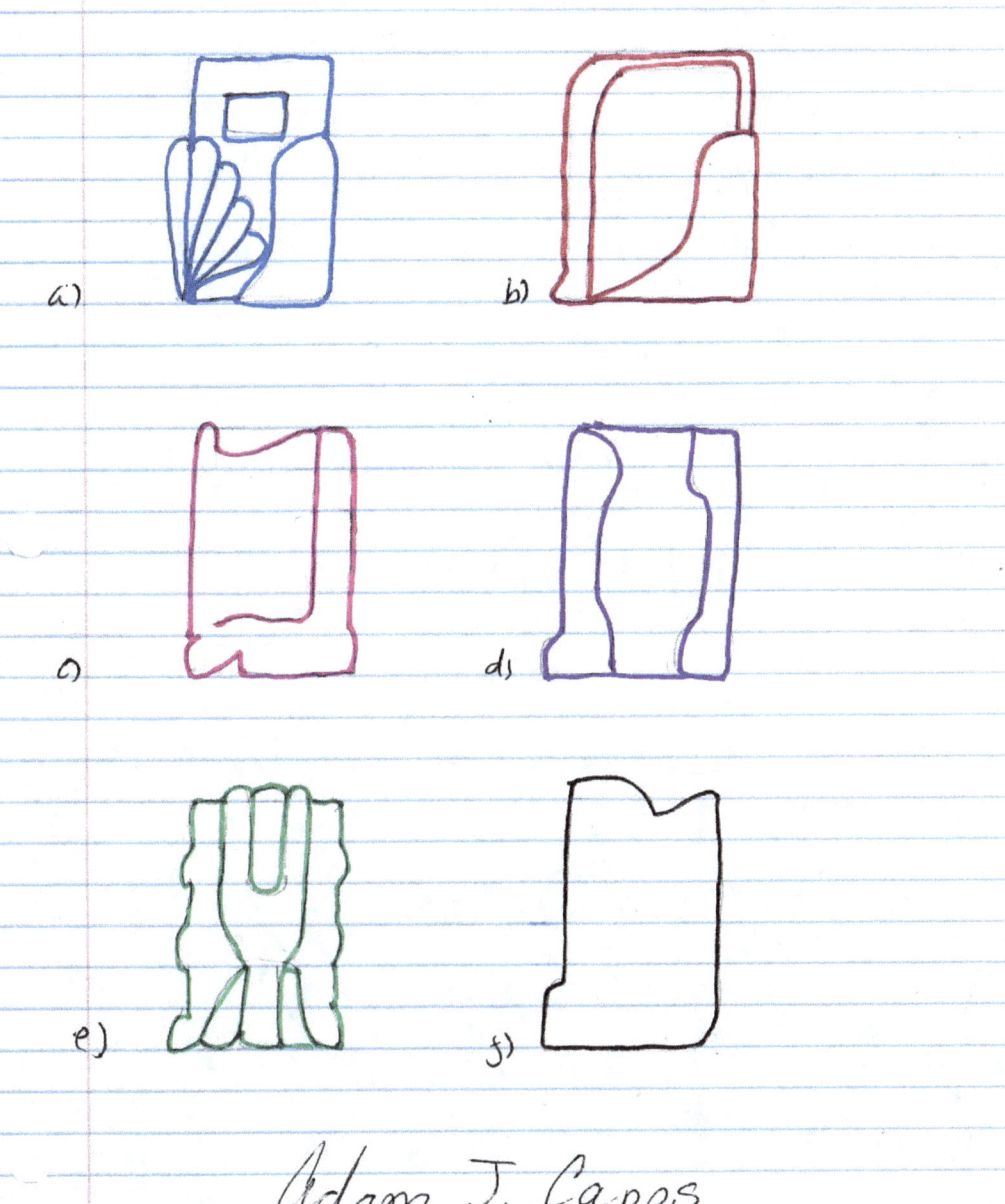

a)

b)

c)

d)

e)

f)

Adam J. Capps

controller designs part 5

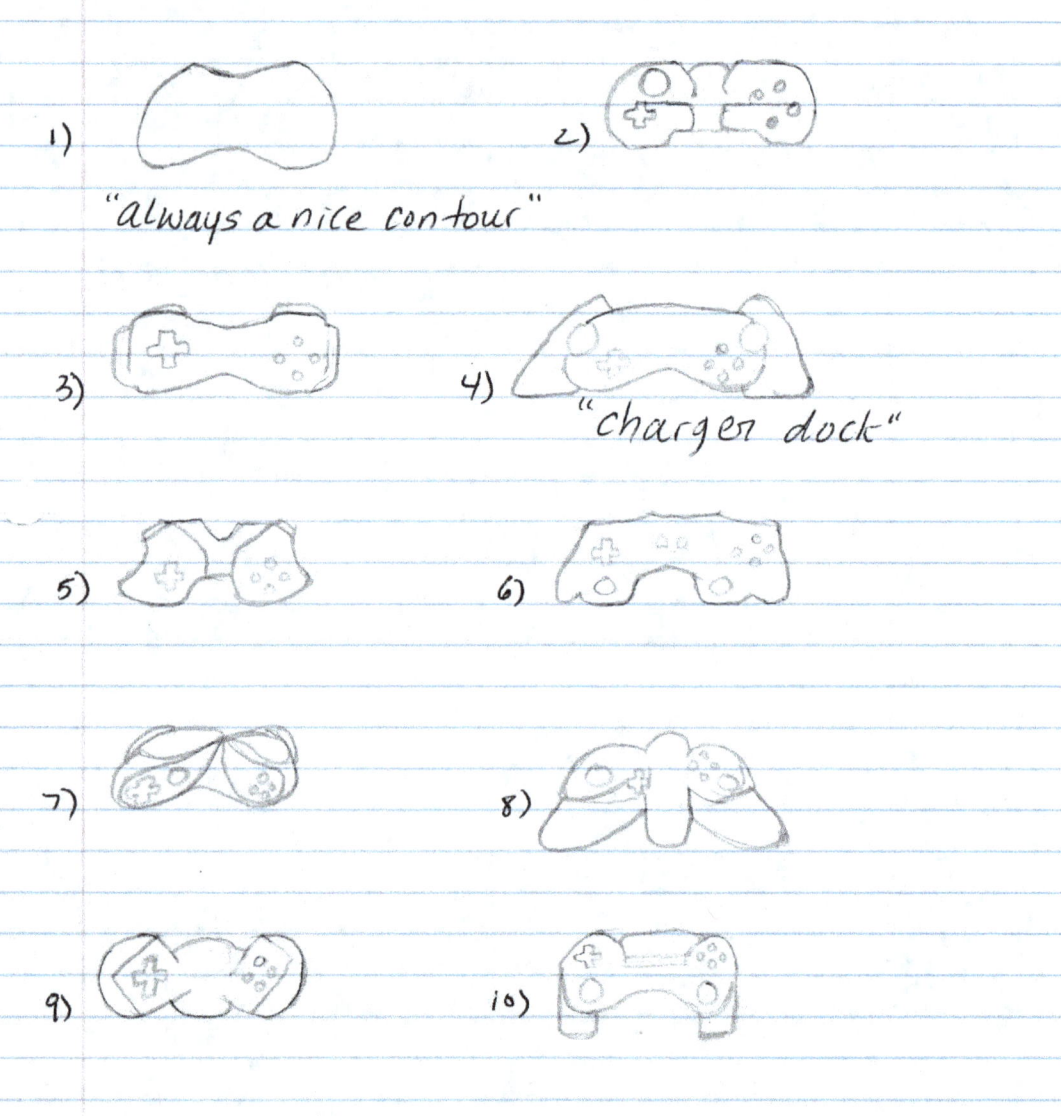

1) "always a nice contour"

2)

3)

4) "charger dock"

5)

6)

7)

8)

9)

10)

LCD Game concepts

1) A double sided portable LCD game.
On one side poker and on the other
slots. Or on one side blackjack
and the other slots. Also, level 2
can be on the other side. Beat
level one then turn it over.

2)

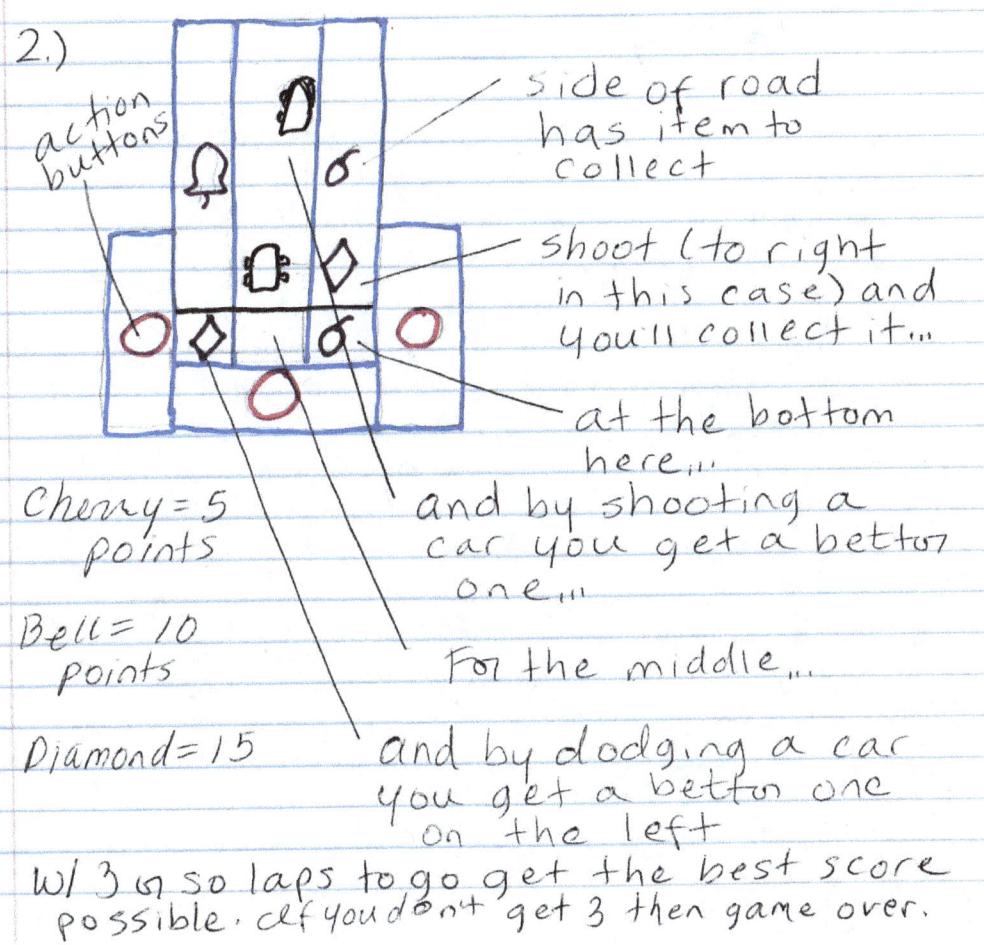

side of road
has item to
collect

shoot (to right
in this case) and
you'll collect it...

at the bottom
here...

and by shooting a
car you get a better
one...

For the middle...

and by dodging a car
you get a better one
on the left

Cherry = 5
points

Bell = 10
points

Diamond = 15

w/ 3 or so laps to go get the best score
possible. If you don't get 3 then game over.

LCD Game Concepts 2

A game you could call "spook invaders." Little ghosts gradually come down & you must shoot them w/ a lightning bolt before they reach the bottom. Here there are 3 lights on each side. You see three color buttons at the bottom. When the colors match (they randomly change colors) you can defeat a whole row of ghosts w/ one button press (in this case red.)

Random Ideas

1) Using a hollowgram w/ a tilt mechanism.

2) A switch that changes the action buttons into four other uses, also, they light up red when you do.

3) As we know, watches have indiglo. LCD games use the same digital graphics, so can be added to those.

4) Like a Nintendo 64 controller only the bottom middle has a digital display screen:

press this button to change between things on a smaller screen, for this portable system idea.

Adam Capps'
Football Game concept

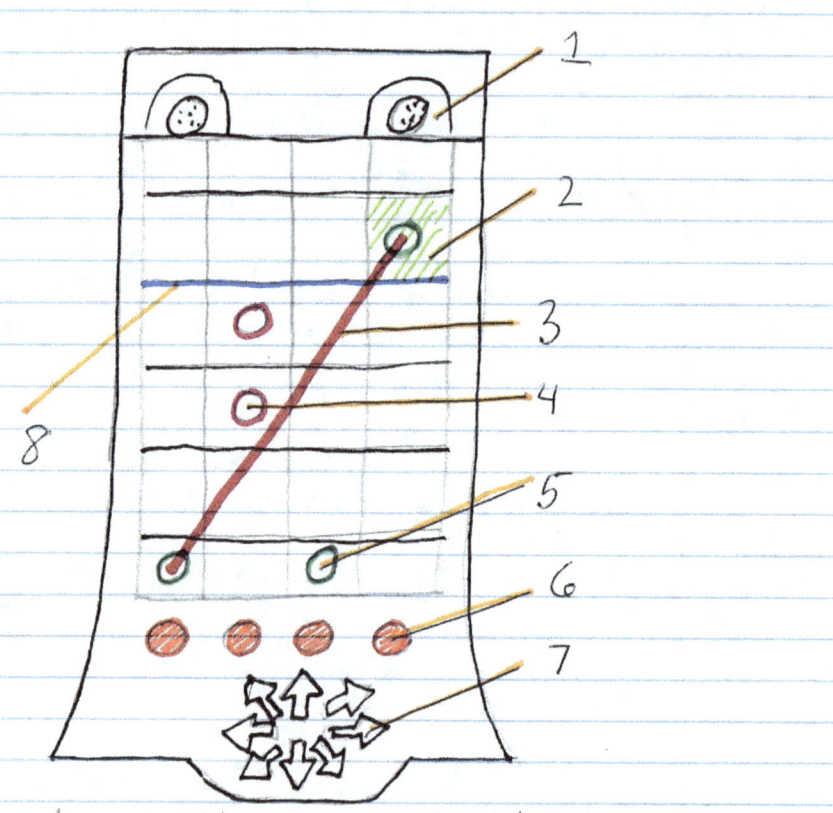

1) speaker either sounds "kick" to the
   left or right. That direction for touchdown.
2) Aim towards indiglo-lit catcher
3) Laser that throws in the direction of input
4) red = other team   5) green = your team

6&7 are throwing direction inputs.

8) a fiber-optic light shows you where
   first down is.

Portable Game Designs

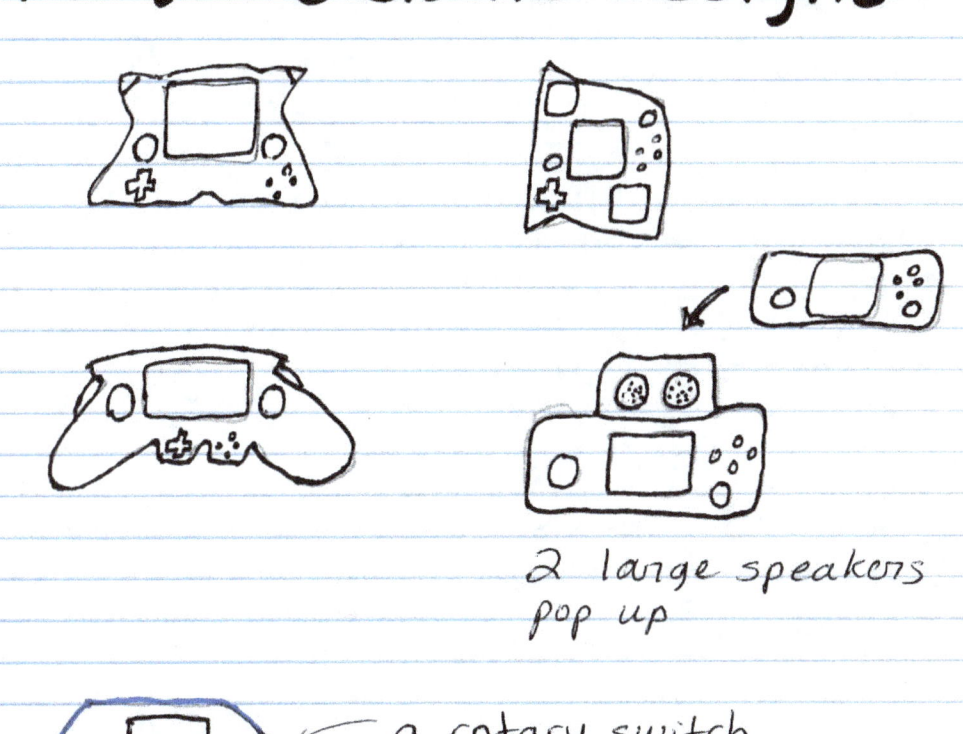

2 large speakers
pop up

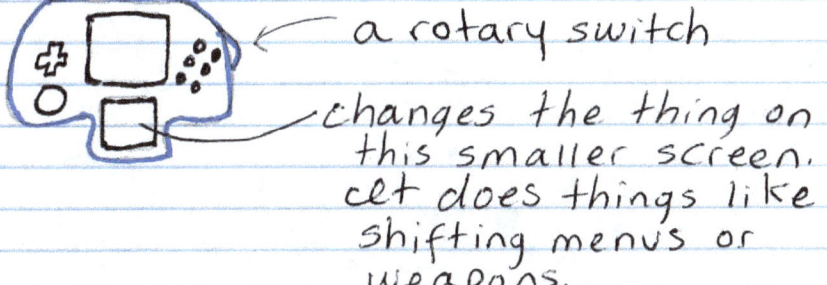

a rotary switch

changes the thing on
this smaller screen.
It does things like
shifting menus or
weapons.

Same concepts only
two smaller screens.
Here those rotary
switches replace the
L & R buttons.

Adam J. Capps

Peripherals

1) An RPG set of peripherals —

 for the magician

 For the Knight

For the Bard

 For the game master

2) In a classic games bundle include a classic controller

3) Gambling game peripherals — slot machine handles, dice & tray in an electronic way, roulette wheel, ect., graphically enhanced.

Light effects

1) Instead of just a power button an image of a moving fire

2) or of a rainbow that changes colors

3.) or an eye opens when the power is turned on...

   maybe w/a red or blue pupil...

4.) Console gloes in the dark

5.) The sides of the console have a graphical effect to them. Maybe you can even change between them.

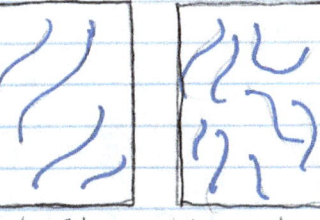

Shifting blue lines

6.) Lights on the console indicate certain game play things. The game turns on a light on the console meaning something.

—Adam J. Capps

wands for any game:

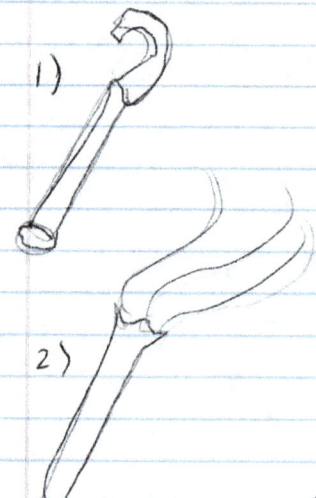

1) Question cane, no telling what it will do next.

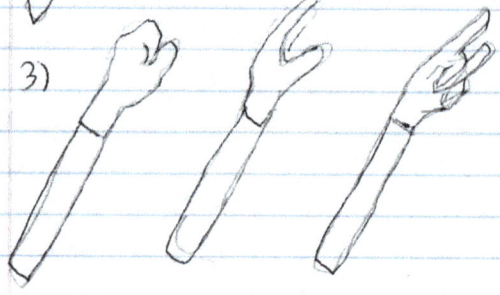

2) Produces smoke, raises a helpful spirit.

3) The hand wand and gestures of magic. A fist hammer, pointed beam, grabs, things like that.

4) A black, gray, and white wand for black, gray, and white magic powers.

Adam Jeremy Capps

Different things that come out of the pipe

or well, or tube, or box...

hand   frog w/ sticky   Fire dragon "pours
              tongue   himself" out

Smoke rings   praying mantus
or just rings.   like creature.
You can float   Don't let it grab
on them!   you!

upward bullet   pacman like ghosts

healing waters or   A fan that
energy boosters   lets you float
of different kinds   upwards.

-Adam Jeremy Capps

Ideas for video games
#3

For shoveling you are given an indication of what could be found. Whitish parts for clay, darker spots for something, glittering dust = magic dust, small twinkeling stones for gems.

Clay makers within the game can mold a helpful idol or helpful creature, until it breaks. maybe it can be repaired at a lower cost.

2.) Special color gems emit a light that has different effects on the surrounding area. Transforming, destroying, giving light, revealing the otherwise invisible, ect.

3.) a double sided sword gives you two power options. During game play select "upper" or "lower."

4.) Look of a "wand sword." Change pentacles/sigils for different powers.

Ideas for video games #4
Weapon Ideas:

1.) The glass sword. It's powerfull, may blast a strong spell on something, but can only be used once as it breaks upon use.

2.) The mirror shield captures enemies. You can do different things w/ them. Carry an enemy to a special place for a special effect, use them against other enemies, combine them into one monster for a greatly grotesque and powerful beast, or just disolve them.

3.) You feed and honor things in the game and the more you do the more they will help and guide you. Feeding the birds & the flying creatures have them surround and protect you. Giving a proper burial for a fallen soldier aids you through his spirit. Tithing to an idol serves you well and so on.

Adam Jeremy Capps

Ideas for video games #5
Random ideas for new games

1.) A classic red devil
as an enemy

2.) At the end of a level or
within a special place
you can get a very special
item if you tip the scales
w/ your gold coins. The
counter balance is a random amount,
a random wieght that can be low if
you are lucky, high if you are not.
If you out weigh that w/ your gold coins
then you get both the prize and your
money back. If you do not then you
lose both the prize and your money.

3.) Foot
sword
enemy

A strange enemy
that jumps around
(watch out for its
spiked boots) And
tries to attack you
w/ its sword.

Adam Jeremy Capps

Literal Game Cube

1)

6 different screens,
6 different games,
position them to play
that game (according to how you
place the cube in the case, the side
facing you is the game that plays.)

2)

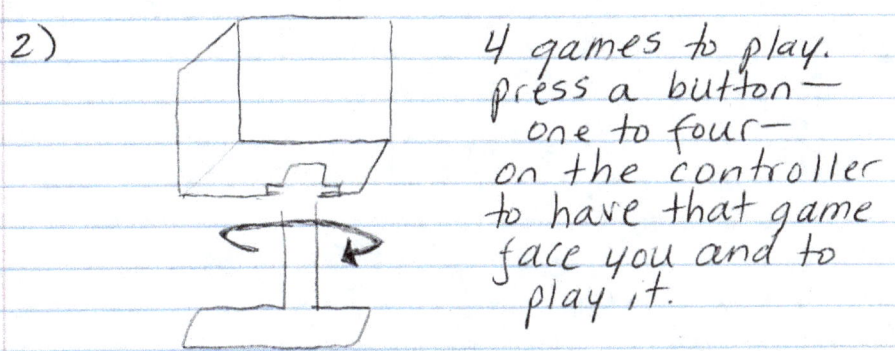

4 games to play.
press a button—
one to four—
on the controller
to have that game
face you and to
play it.

Adam Jeremy Capps

cIdeas for Video Games
#6

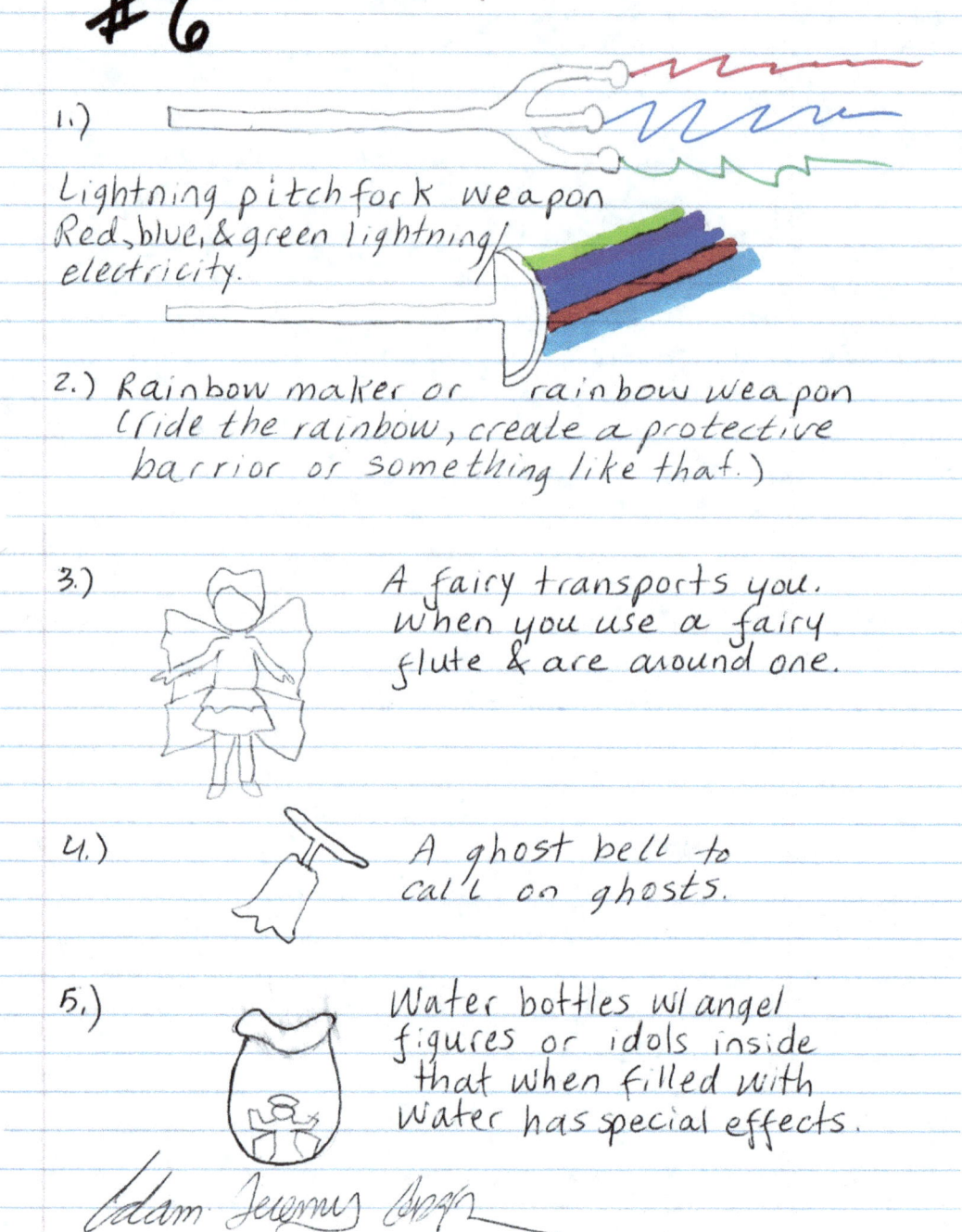

1.) Lightning pitchfork weapon
Red, blue, & green lightning/
electricity.

2.) Rainbow maker or rainbow weapon
(ride the rainbow, create a protective
barrior or something like that.)

3.) A fairy transports you.
When you use a fairy
flute & are around one.

4.) A ghost bell to
call on ghosts.

5.) Water bottles w/ angel
figures or idols inside
that when filled with
water has special effects.

Ideas for Video Games - 7

1) in every town you can be baptized,
for a fee. It randomly raises
certain stats until you die.

2.) In a hidden place in the level

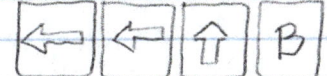

you see one of these randomly generated
codes. you use the code at the end
of the level to enter into a bonus level.
You can put such a thing in different
genres of games, too.

3.) Simularly, in a dungeon of an adventure
game, you fight 4 mini bosses ((could
be just 3) and after each one is
defeated an input is placed on the
door of the final boss. When you
get all three they all appear and
can be inputed to enter.

And other ways such a thing can be
used: Like in a cart game while
racing through an upper part shows
the input code. You might have to
reveal the input code w/a special
item, and so on.

Adam Jeremy Capps

Ideas for video Games # 8

1)

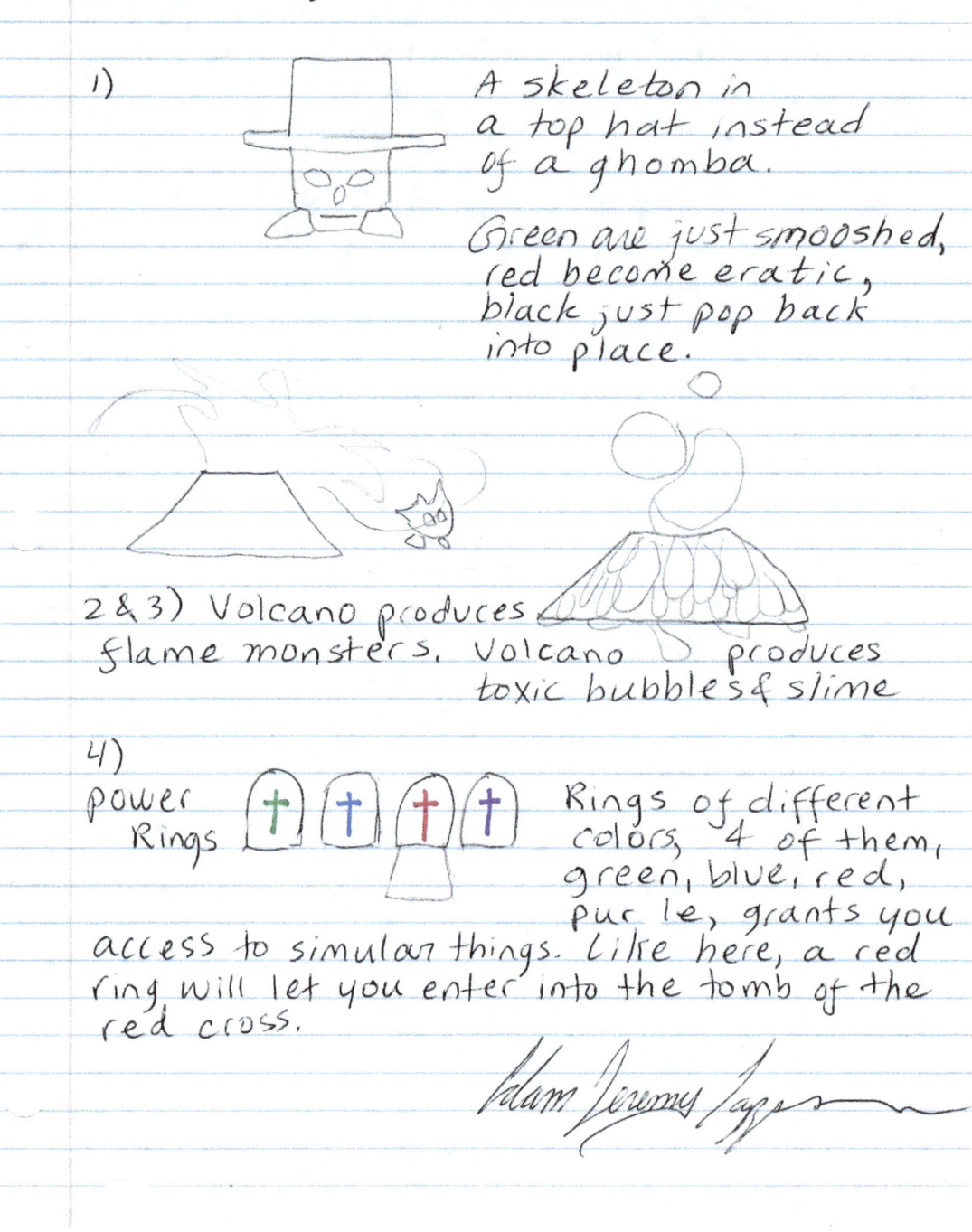

A skeleton in a top hat instead of a ghomba.

Green are just smooshed, red become eratic, black just pop back into place.

2 & 3) Volcano produces flame monsters. Volcano produces toxic bubbles & slime

4)

power Rings

Rings of different colors, 4 of them, green, blue, red, purle, grants you access to simular things. Like here, a red ring will let you enter into the tomb of the red cross.

Adam Jeremy Capps

Video Game Ideas #9

1) The secrets key lets you into a room that reveals secrets within the game, for things that would be too cryptic otherwise. It could be gotten in one level and the next, before it starts, will display a page that reveals things to you.

2) w/ powerups a flying creature might dive down and take it from you. making them larger, giving them breathing fire, according to what the powerup would have done.

3)

You can add melodies to the games music w/ these "power-ups." If you find the flute within the game a flute melody will be added to the level.

Adam Jeremy Capps

1) The game allows you to tithe to one spirit-god or another. After a certain unknown amount is tithed (a randomly generated number) you will recieve something special. There is a small chance it will not take a lot but a greater chance it will.

2)

You Have

A use of points [5] towards these POINTS as shown:

Add power to

Fire, lightning, air, water

defense

Magic defense

And you can add more tiles by obtaining them (such as for an increase in strength, speed, other stats, and so on.)

Adam Jeremy Capps

Game Ideas # 11
My Mega Men

1.) Slime man   2.) Tornado man

3.) Steam man   4.) Fungus man

5.) Grind man   6.) Claw man

                    8.) pumpkin man

7.) Cloak man

Ideas for games #12

1.) There is a hole you can only go down if a rabbit does first — which is a rare and random occurance.

2.) 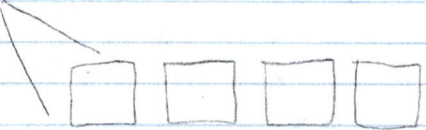 Regular bombs but also blue water bombs. Bombs that can be thrown into water.

3.)

A bomb that splits into four

4.)

Areas where a light shines upon something depending on the time of day. When you arive one will be shined down on and you will recieve something accordingly.

Adam Jeremy Capps

Ideas for Games # 13

1.) A right of passage thing. If you are not worthy to pass then light-ning will de-stroy you.

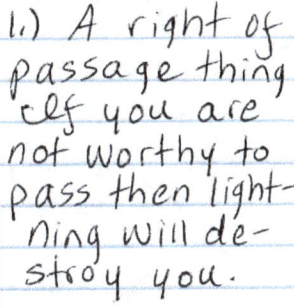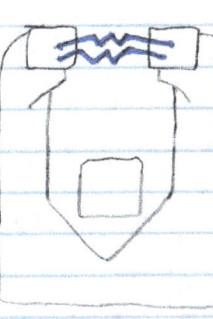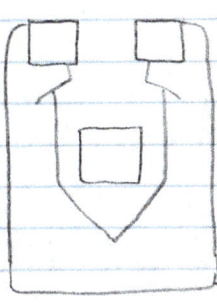

As seen in the first drawing. However, if you are worthy of passing through you will get a special item or power when you stand on the square. This is the overhead perspective of that.

2.) You find a box of keys, like a hundred keys & suddenly have access to a lot of things— doors, chests. It might be found in a ghost town, in the castle of a fallen kingdom, or a many corridor place where dwarves once lived.

3.) There is four or even sometimes 6 levels of flying. The weakest flying power up only takes you to the first upper level, the next flying power-up to the second and so on.

Adam J. Capps

no. 14-
Some more video game ideas
from Adam Jeremy Capps

1) A powerup that lets you pass through nearly anything. Like in an RPG instead of fleeing you just walk right pass the enemy.

2.) A remote control weapon, open boxes that drop down things on your enemy. Turn on or off lights (turn them off if it helps you from being seen), turn on the light of a star to defeat nightly creatures, operate machinery with the remote & so on.

3.) Obtain the power of the 5 images. These images are shown from place to place throughout the game. Once you've obtained one they will help you in the area they are shown. If you get the sword image and find that image in an area then in that area your sword will become more powerful. If you get the star image then in the areas you see them stars will burst out and destroy all the enemies.

Adam Jeremy Capps's
Video Game Ideas # 15

1.) electric boots

Shock your enemy on any metallic platform or shocking water/pools.

Operate machinery by giving it electricity. Such as a double wing platform, by giving it electricity it flaps its wings.

Stomp on enemies you otherwise couldn't.

2.) The hammer boot. Kick down just about anything.

3.) The reflect shield. Refflects your enemies' attacks back at them.

4.) Fairy dust that pixel-ates enemies

5.) Bombs that don't blast but instead have things burst out and all around. Special tiles to place bombs on w/ an image on them to tell you what will happen if you do — or magical stones for the same idea.

Video Game Ideas #16

The plug wand — plug it in something w/ different effects.

Sometimes for energy or magic boosts,

Sometimes to produce something special, like from a brick.

2. Tithing to gods — there are four prayers to select from first such as "pray for a better weapon," or "pray for a new spell," then you tithe. Only after you've tithed a good amount will that come true.

3.) Instead of a thwomp (mario) an upside down star. It opens its udjat/ eye of Horus like eye & comes down on you.

4.) The more black magic you use the more power is stored up for white magic and vice versa.

Adam Jeremy Cappa

Video Game Ideas # 17

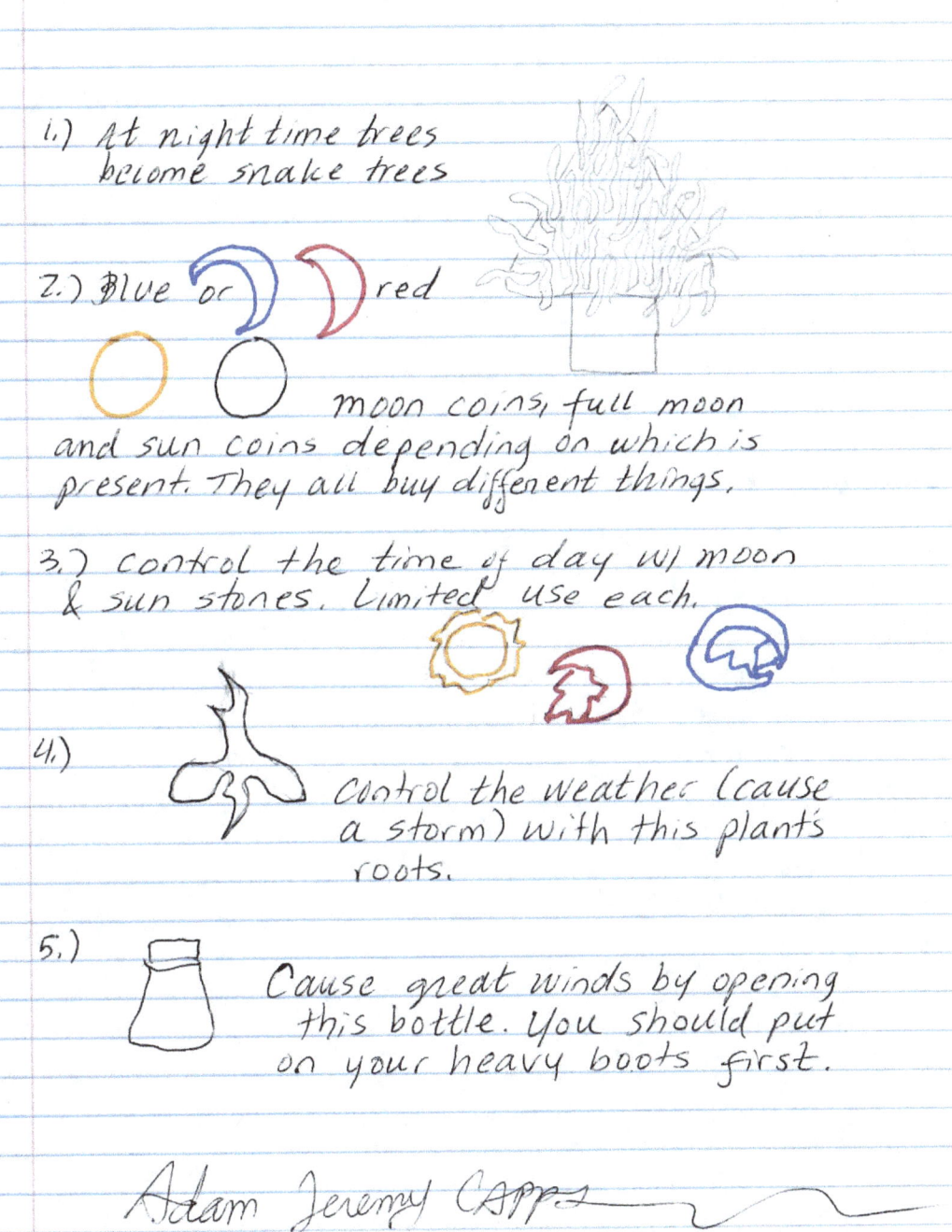

1.) At night time trees become snake trees

2.) Blue or red

moon coins, full moon and sun coins depending on which is present. They all buy different things.

3.) Control the time of day w/ moon & sun stones. Limited use each.

4.) Control the weather (cause a storm) with this plants roots.

5.) Cause great winds by opening this bottle. You should put on your heavy boots first.

Adam Jeremy Capps

Video Game Ideas # 18

1) Some cannons will shoot out coins after you jump on top of them, as a switch.

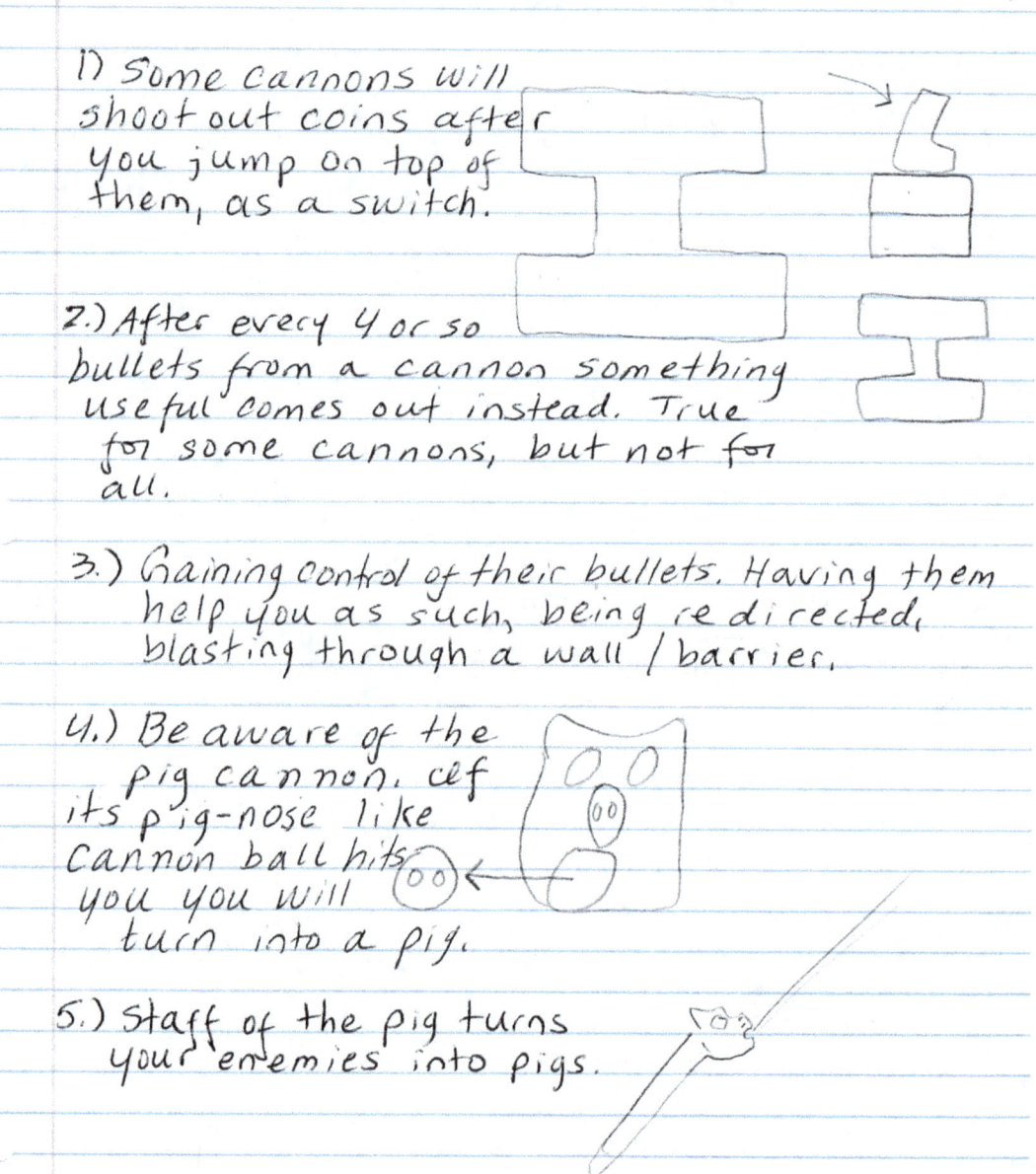

2.) After every 4 or so bullets from a cannon something useful comes out instead. True for some cannons, but not for all.

3.) Gaining control of their bullets. Having them help you as such, being redirected, blasting through a wall / barrier.

4.) Be aware of the pig cannon. If its pig-nose like cannon ball hits you you will turn into a pig.

5.) Staff of the pig turns your enemies into pigs.

Adam Goggin

Video Game ideas # 19

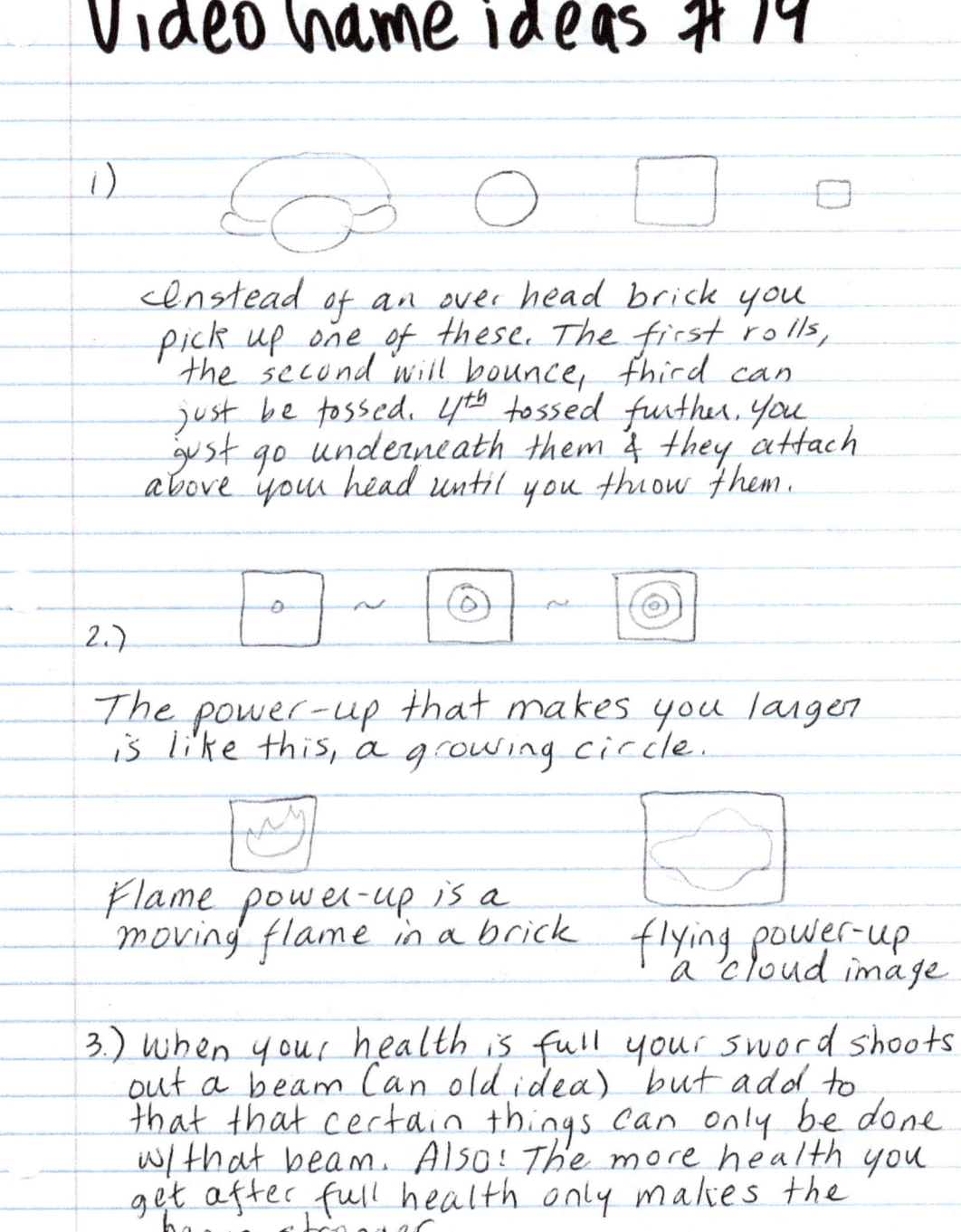

1)

Instead of an over head brick you pick up one of these. The first rolls, the second will bounce, third can just be tossed. 4th tossed further. You just go underneath them & they attach above your head until you throw them.

2.)

The power-up that makes you larger is like this, a growing circle.

Flame power-up is a moving flame in a brick

flying power-up a cloud image

3.) When your health is full your sword shoots out a beam (an old idea) but add to that that certain things can only be done w/ that beam. Also! The more health you get after full health only makes the beam stronger.

Video Game Ideas #20

1.) 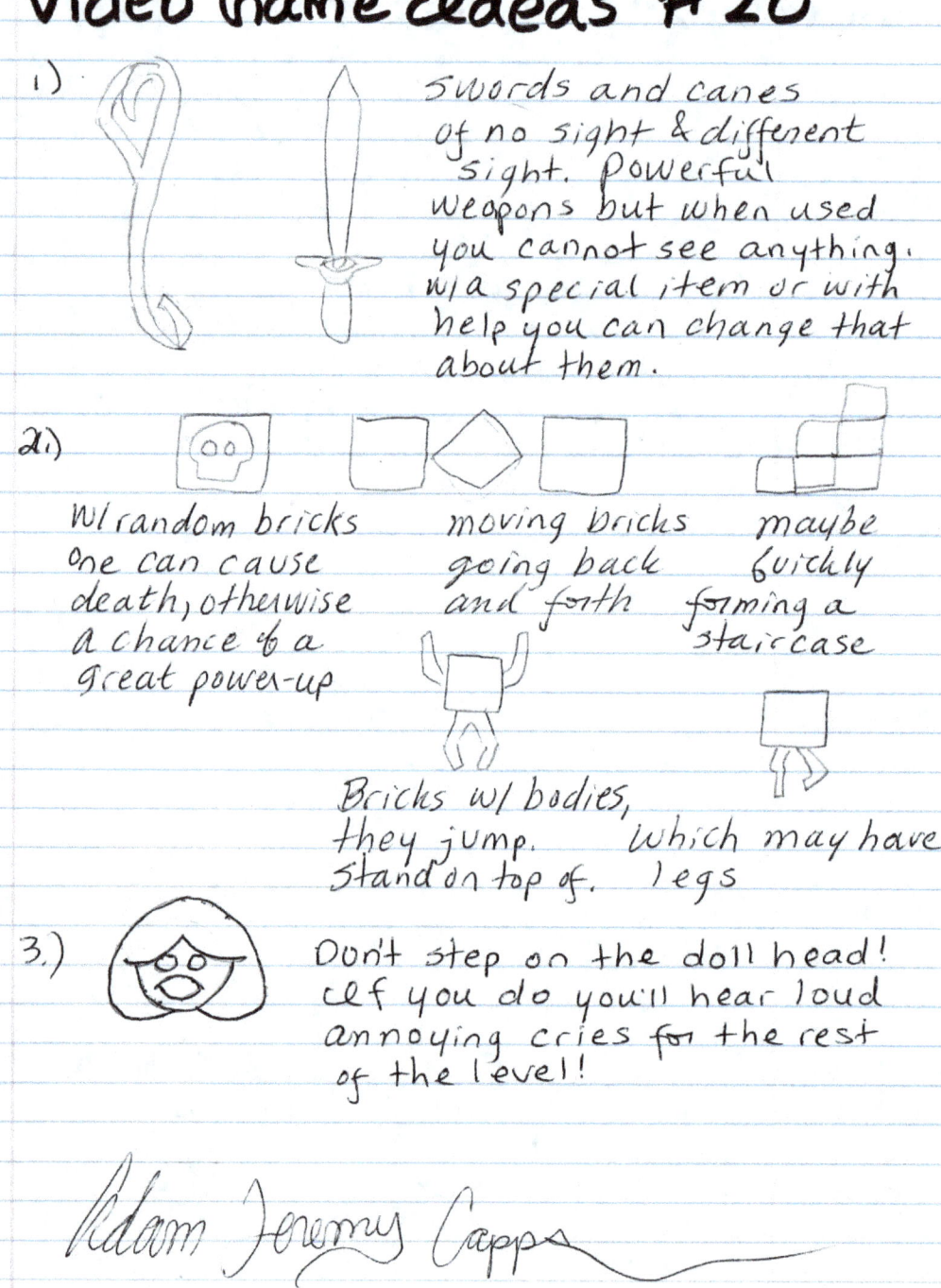 Swords and canes of no sight & different sight. Powerful weapons but when used you cannot see anything. w/ a special item or with help you can change that about them.

2.) w/ random bricks one can cause death, otherwise a chance of a great power-up

moving bricks going back and forth

maybe quickly forming a staircase

Bricks w/ bodies, they jump. Stand on top of.

Which may have legs

3.) Don't step on the doll head! If you do you'll hear loud annoying cries for the rest of the level!

Adam Jeremy Capps

Video Game Ideas #21

1.) Warp zone idea.

2.) The
rotating
heart

Upright is health, downward is damage

3. plants
growing
quickly w/
seeds but
only if you put the seeds in a special
pot. Grow different things according to
the pot, not the seed.

4.) in a platforming
game if you   shoot something
                     w/an arrow & it
                     falls below into
                     a basket
then something special will happen.

Video game ideas #22

1.) 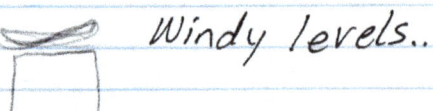 a fan on a pipe (or your equivelent of a pipe.) when it spins it'll damage you, otherwise you can jump on it.

Windy levels..

2.) my alternative idea for a ball and chain (ala SMB3)

A fan brick & basket.

3.)

When you die your sword gains wings, flies to a stone, planting itself into it, where you are reborn.

Adam Cozzen

Video game ideas # 23

1.) you have a volatile weapon so be careful how you use it.

2.)

step on the squishy ball, it pours acid over a brick, disolving it, opening a lower area to you.

3. Coin operated elevator. cln this case it'll send you up w/ 20 coins.

4.)

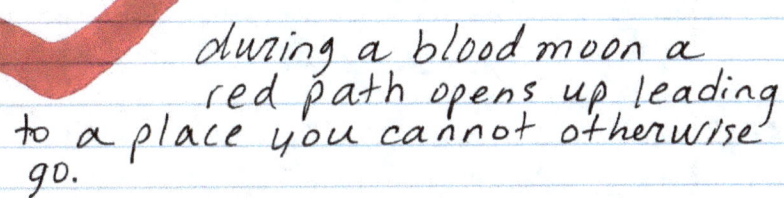

during a blood moon a red path opens up leading to a place you cannot otherwise go.

Video game ideas #24

1.)

Wand of the skulls

Wand of the bats

2.)

Slime ball cannon

3. Goat shoes ▢ for zipping around on the mountain

Adam Jeremy Capps

New video game ideas #25

1.) Every 5 levels you level up

Select something to show it.
- an armband, pink feather,
green belt/headband. The
color shows what level you are.

2.) A vehicle to ride
on:

← spike boots

↳ seat

3.) "shadow of the
evil tree."
Don't stand
in its shadow!

It will turn you into an evil beast.
Then again the game could make
that a good thing, giving you temporary
power from tree to tree.

Adam J. Capps

cIdeas for video games #26

1.) A guy in a cloud has a net & tries to scoop you up when
you jump

2.) A "spirit" meter. you can transform into a spirit for
as many bars you have. One thing you can do as a spirit is fly, or go down a small hole to reach a lower area.

3.) 3 crowns above your head. maybe things

can't harm you from above or maybe they attach to an upper thing and bring it down.

4.)

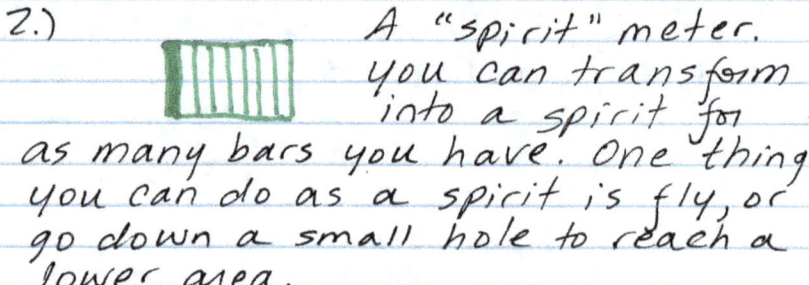

A flame above your head. You charge it (holding down a button) until it goes from a small flame to a powerful large fire.

Adam Jeremy Capps

video game ideas # 27

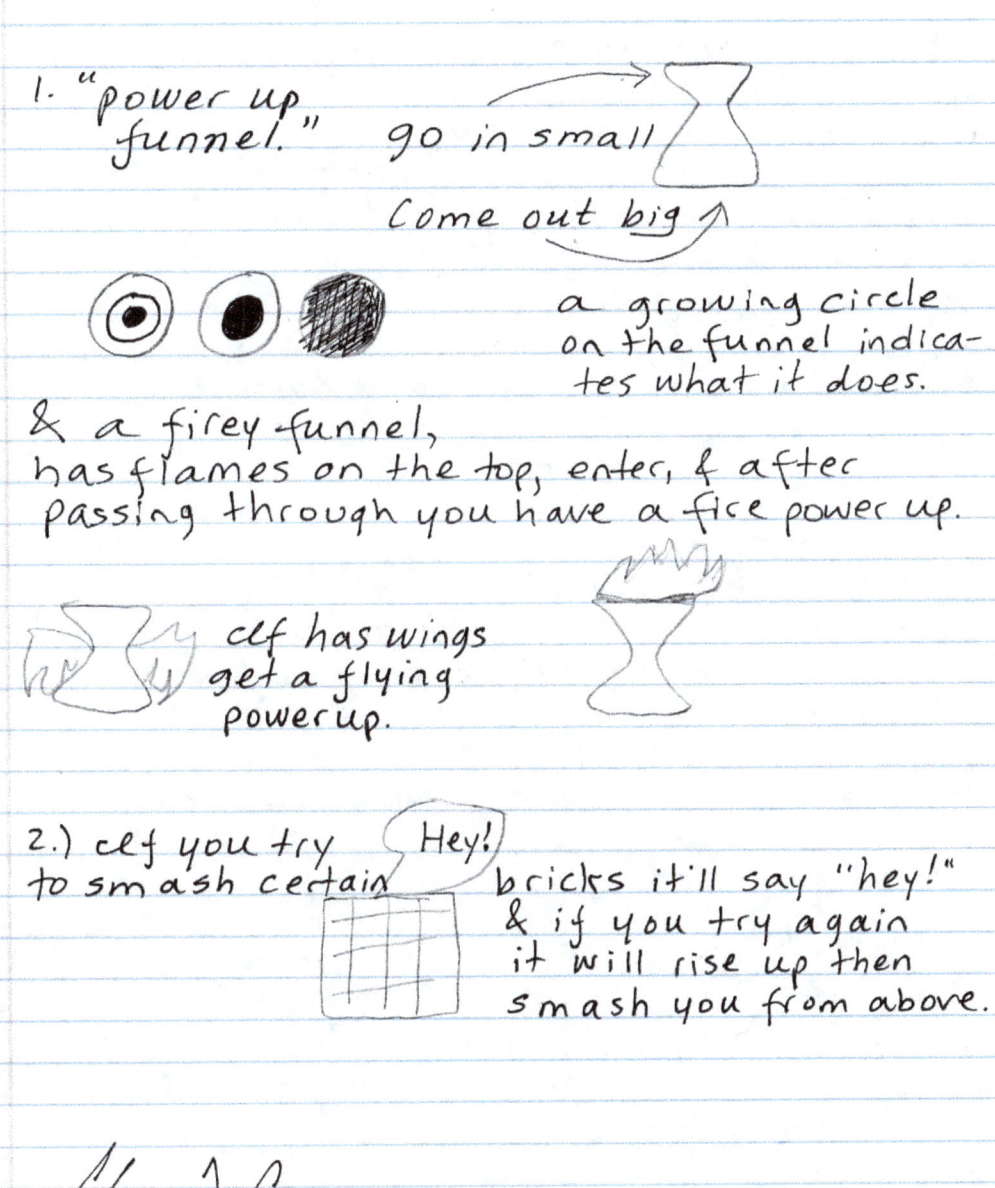

1. "power up funnel." go in small

Come out big

a growing circle on the funnel indicates what it does.

& a firey funnel, has flames on the top, enter, & after passing through you have a fire power up.

clf has wings get a flying power up.

2.) clf you try to smash certain ~~Hey!~~ bricks it'll say "hey!" & if you try again it will rise up then smash you from above.

Adam J. Cappa

Video game ideas #28

1.) Gain extra energy from an eye above that drops tears below

2.) A mouth opens and a rope comes down—which you can climb.

3.) harmful snot from a nose. Or maybe snakes come out.

4.) A mouth producing a bloody waterfall.

maybe vampiric looking

Adam Jeremy Capps

New video game ideas #29

1.) defeat a mouse & get a mouse cursor for whatever useful purpose

Defeat a difficult cat & get 9 lives. Dogs or wolves on a leash may protect you— like in an RPG when you don't want to be bothered with random battles.

2.) A skull mask as a weapon. cet shoots out firey skulls

3.) sponge shoes take whatever fluid you step on and give it any number of effects to what you step on afterwards.

4.) Hit the "home" brick & you may go back to your home, get something, then return to the level.

Adam Jeremy Capps

New video game ideas #30

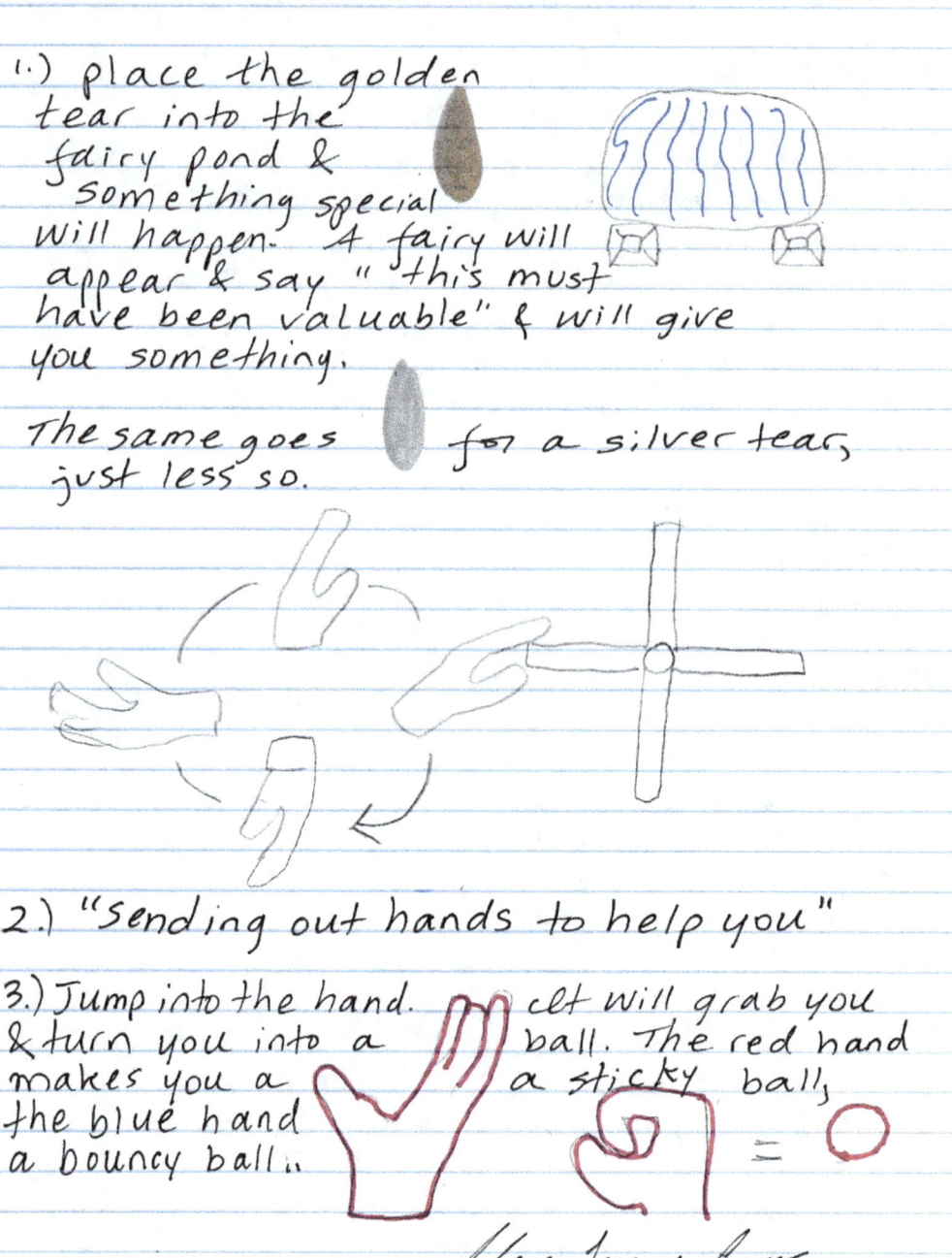

1.) place the golden tear into the fairy pond & something special will happen. A fairy will appear & say " this must have been valuable" & will give you something.

The same goes for a silver tear, just less so.

2.) "sending out hands to help you"

3.) Jump into the hand. It will grab you & turn you into a ball. The red hand makes you a sticky ball, the blue hand a bouncy ball.

Adam Jeremy Capps

Video Game Ideas #31

1.) 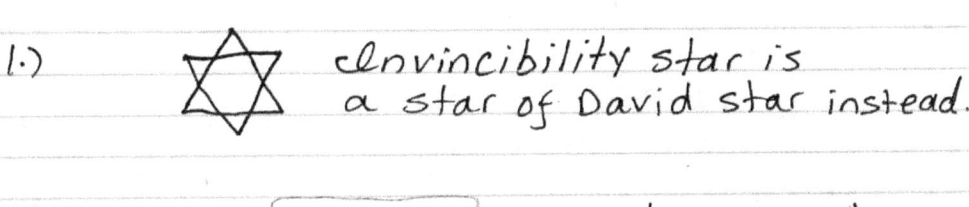 Invincibility star is a star of David star instead.

2.) Treasure chests slide open   or have a glass top that requires a strong hammer to break & get inside

And may have a hole going downward. Smoke may pour out from those not allowing you to enter w/o a special mask.

Maybe they have such heavy lids that you need a strength gauntlet to open them.

They might be invisible requiring a special tool to see.
You might have to light a candle to the left & right of them before it can be opened.

Then their could be a vending machine kind of thing to them only they require special coins or maybe special stones.

- AJC

Video Game Ideas # 32

1.) magical vests turn you into things. This one a skeleton.

Just jump on top of.

2.) A power up that lets you "swim in the air." A powerup that lets you walk & jump regularly within the water.

3. The last spot at the end of the level is a cloudy storm.

Lightning strikes you tuning you into an upward going bolt, you enter upward into a cloud that sends you to the next level.

& if you get the blue bolt ⚡ within the level then your energy will be restored for the next. ⚡ getting the green bolt is a hidden exit.

Adam Jeremy Capps

Video game ideas # 33

1.) Mini bonus room idea. During the level you can find a red, green, and blue coin. They fall into their own slot. That slot turns into a basket (as seen w/ the red coin below.) Then things fall from above & whatever lands in your basket (s) is what you get.

2. Walking cannon guy.

sun ball

dragon head ball

← gains wings

goes up high then bothers you from above. 8 ball is fortune if you jump on top of it.

New video game ideas # 34

1.) You burn his fire, he opens comes out of   pipe w/ magical his eyes & smoke his nose.

2.) Combine two things into 1 w/ this wand. Or separate one thing into two in a useful way — or bring 2 things together

3.) placing a certain crown on the head of this statue will cause an   evil being to rise. A king does so thinking that being would give him power for it.

Adam Jeremy Capps

New video game ideas # 35

1.) The magical net catches things that are invisible.

Just swing it and there's no telling what you'll get.

2. A sign stops you from going any further. It is one of The king's (or Queen's) signs w/an ever watching eye on it. So the only way you will be able to pass is by turning invisible & you will need something for that.

DO NOT PASS

3.) Spider shoes — climb up just about anything. Can be more tentacle like

Could help you underwater

Adam Jeremy Capps

Video Game Ideas # 36

1.) A trick spring leading right into a monster's mouth.

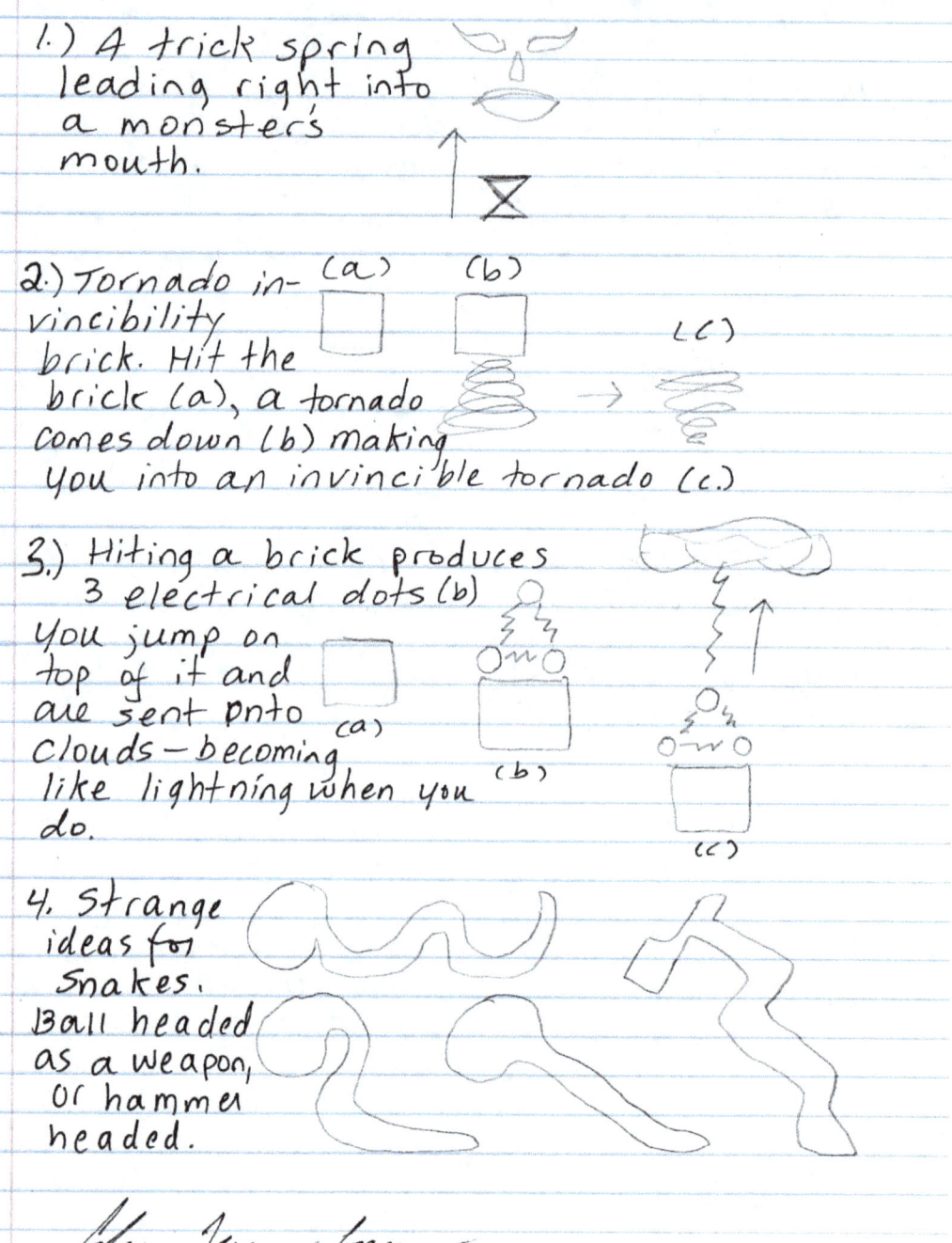

2.) Tornado invincibility brick. Hit the brick (a), a tornado comes down (b) making you into an invincible tornado (c.)

(a)   (b)   (c)

3.) Hiting a brick produces 3 electrical dots (b) You jump on top of it and are sent onto clouds – becoming like lightning when you do.

(a)   (b)   (c)

4. Strange ideas for snakes. Ball headed as a weapon, or hammer headed.

Video game ideas #37

1.) Hat that sends out rings as weapons, sort of like a halo.

Also: Flame on top, star on top, smoke, or whatever else.

2.) The double sided brick. you can only smash one or the other to get something, but not both, so guess right (unless you've already figured it out.)

3. A "random" brick. Hitting it makes a hand appear. The hand's thumb goes up & down over and over again landing on one or the other. Thumbs up gives you something good. Thumbs down denies you.

4. A black hole to either leave the level or to enter into a hidden level.

New Video Game ideas #37

1.) A D-pad 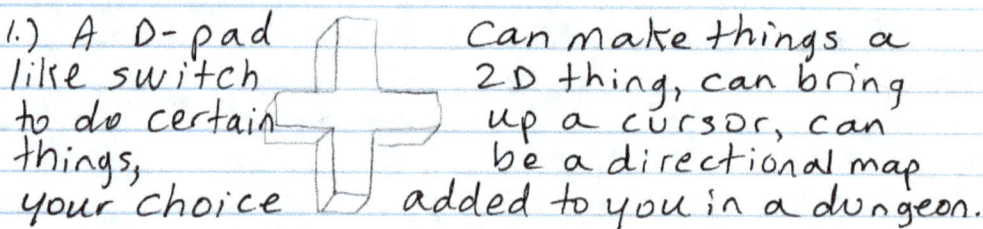 Can make things a
like switch 2D thing, can bring
to do certain up a cursor, can
things, be a directional map
your choice added to you in a dungeon.

2.) A roll
out bridge
as a tool,
or a pad of some kind. Not only to go
over pits but fire as well.

3.) Like one of those new year's day

whistles, where the end rolls out.
Use it anywhere to bring up a rolled
out bridge. (The whistle itself isn't the
bridge.)

4.) Making the basis of tools and
weapons kid's toys.

5.) The only thing blocking your
way is a hanging cloth — a
magical one. But w/a magical
candle you can burn it away.

Adam Jeremy Capps

Video Game Ideas #39

1.) A "guess a number between 1 and 5" thing. Maybe you can win more guesses.

2.) A star switch makes it day. A moon switch makes it night.

3.) Look of powerup that stops time. It appears on screen turning around until you stop it. or

4.) In a difficult (otherwise difficult) level you can throw something in the gears of this clock to freeze time in the level.

5.) Like a wolf/dog sled only

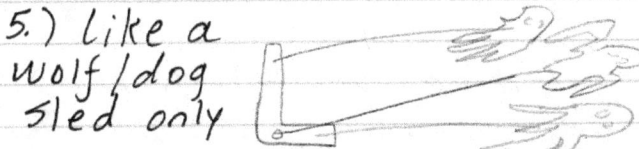

one for underwater travel, guided by squids instead of dogs.

Adam Jeremy Capps

Video Game Ideas # 40

1.)
"Ghost sled"

Or maybe riding upward on ghosts by standing on them. Maybe at a graveyard after you have summoned one.

2.) Jump off of any clif w/a prote tive orb. Enter into a protective orb & you can shoot yourself through a cannon. It starts w/a magic green marble. By doing certain things w/ it in the game it gets larger & larger until you can enter inside.

3.) The field of magical swords. Many power- full swords placed into tree trunks in a very special area of the game.

4.) The eternal flame & the six candles. Depending on which one you light something special happens, something to keep forever, But you can only light one.

Video Game Ideas #41

1.) When you hit a dandelion fairies come out.

2.) You hit a brick for a power up, but when it (a mushroom or something edible) comes out, a frog takes it from you with its tongue. Then maybe it gets larger or something and hops away. Or maybe it spits it out and something improved comes out.

3.) power to turn things upside down: you could flip a platform dropping you down to a lower area. You could flip an upper platform that drops a rope when you do, and climb it.

You can flip the image shown. This is above you and one cup restores energy, another contains something else, as poured out. Or a helpful item from above could be brought down.

Video Game Ideas # 42

1. A magical room w/ a knob on its door, creating/sending you to 8 different rooms or places.

2. Safety tiles are a regular thing you can get. Or you place them on top of a cube (3) to have something come out. maybe for crossing a hole. maybe if you get enough you can create a magical archway as so: you see if you have enough to do so when they go from black to blue on the items screen.

3. Secret revealing trumpet. It sends out rings & if the rings bounce back then there is a secret there (secret entryway, chest, something hidden.)

4.) loud pitched whistle that breaks glass. maybe causing shards to fall down on your enemy. maybe to get through a window.

Adam J Coppo

Video Game Ideas #43

1.) An elastic star sort of weapon:

above the player's head.

2.) "Wing staff."

3.) Scorpion-like monster

4.) A thunderstorm rolls around on different levels, randomly moving about. Like in a Super Mario Bros. 3 world map. If it lands on a level you enter then there will be a windy storm in that level.

Adam Capps

Video Game Ideas # 44

1.) on the world map two routes —
the long & easy or the short & difficult.

2.) Sometimes, randomly, there are
black clouds above & flying up upon
them sends you to a strange place.

3.)

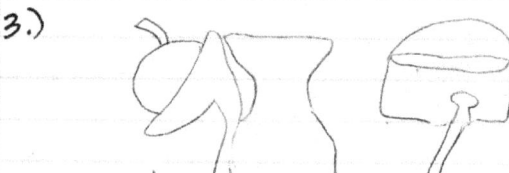

Special axe to
cut the cord,
moving it otherwise
will blow it up.

the only way to break the vase & take
the things inside is by placing in a bomb.
Or maybe doing so produces a powerful
upward going beam, dangerous maybe,
or perhaps useful.

4.) Making money highly complex. Different
gems & metals, jewelry production, coin
making w/ magical stamps to press on
a valuable image, gathering, mixing,
w/a sort of alchemy behind it. & bringing
value & added value to just about
anything.

New Video Game Ideas # 45

1.) magical crown you earn which
allows you to attach
5 pieces of magic gems
boosting the power behind
your job.

And just about
anything can have
added power/ability
w/ the gems attached
to them.

2.)
Idols   moving them into a
                           new area, a
                        sacred place
              or something like that,
              is difficult but worth-
              while, bringing you power
&blessings. However, other gods will oppose
you trespassing & replacing them where their
idols reside.

3.) For whatever you buy you can buy
a single dice, too, if you want.
It possibly adds to the value of
what you just bought. #1 or 2 = no
change, # 6 would be high change.

~ Adam Capps

Video Game Ideas #46

1.) Record player plays
   hard music (like metal)
   says something about
   getting you, maybe
   sings in a cheesy way
   "I'm going to get you," record
   stops, disk comes out & attacks you.

2.) Video faces
& video flowers

3.) Releasing fireflys you caught
   and release at night in a special
   place causes something special to
   happen.

4.) Weapon you charge.
Charge (by holding
down button) to make 1   2
a white yin-yang piece.   That one
heals you. Continue holding down the
attack button and a black yin-yang
appears, which will attack enemies.

                                    —Adam J.C.

Video Game Ideas #47

1.) A charge weapon of a  honing missle. The longer you charge it the more missles appear above your head, up to three perhaps. Then release the charge button and they will be used.

2.) strike out the candles w/a skull in between to destroy all skeletal enemies on the screen.

3.) A rare item in the game, a scroll that lets you choose "no more of ( )," where one enemy is removed from the game (other than enemy bosses.)

4.) Electrical arms enemy. cIf they make contact w/ you you get shocked

5.) or sticky balls, or electrical ones.

New video Game Ideas # 48

1.) Magical tuning
forks tell you
where certain things
are. Can come in
the form of a necklace.
Cheap ones show you where crystals
are. Cost more ones, silver. The expensive
ones (made of gold) tell you where gold
is.

2.) You can buy the probability of something from a "chance fortune maker,"
a sort of magician that can turn odds
around. As such you can make money
more likely to come about — even
from a stranger in a villiage, or
find things in the game that otherwise
have very low odds of ever appearing.

3.) There are two orbs,
one of more money &
the other less, when
you get one you will get re-occuring
money once a day for a certain
ammount of game days.

4.) money in denominations,
however the highest (purple)
does an extra thing, not
just giving you money.

5 10 15 20
+...

Video Game Ideas #49

1.) plant shooting out plant:

sometimes they land
& a vine comes up from them.

2.) you bomb away
stones revealing a
mirror, and when
you stand before
it you are doubled, like a shadow,
one that mirrors what you do.

3.) Same idea but with different things

inside. Shown are: treasure chest,
magical light, a sword, and a trapped
fairy— help her & she'll help you.

Video Game Ideas #50

1.) A weapon of a sword that turns & lands on one of four arrows. If it lands on an upper arrow you lose the sword. If left then it attacks the enemy. If it lands on the right it harms you & if it lands on down then it goes back to you doing nothing but made more powerful for the next time.

2.) Magic coin & medallion makers — the choice of gods, prayers, spells, and magic symbols. Enhance w/ gems, maybe obtaining the metals & gems yourself. You may be surprised in the game with how valuable one thing is w/ one person but not another — and a sect of shiva would highly value your coin/medallion while the sect of leviathan wants nothing to do w/ it. Strange & mysterious properties can occur with them too, in an unexpected way.

2.) miniture sword head-piece or miniture sword wand shoots out mini swords.

Adam Jeremy Capps

Video Game Ideas # 51

1.) You can pray... anywhere. Praying in some places, before something — could be anything : a cross, an idol, gravestone, tree, causes a magical thing to happen.

Maybe as well you can gain more prayers throughout the game. Such as "a prayer for spirits," "a prayer for fortune," "a prayer for shiva."

2.) You can buy tripple jumps or you can find them as power ups. You get a certain ammount, what you find or buy. So a power up might give you 10 of them (jump midair 3 times for 10 times.) And simular things w/ dashing, pounding, the difference is you get a certain but definite ammount instead of losing them when you are hit.

3.) In one game you get to a lower level by going down a pipe. In this one you do so by jumping down from a high area and smashing down when you land. The floor may be cracked showing you where it may be done.

— Adam Jeremy Capps

Video Game Ideas # 52

1.) A guitar hero looking thing for an RPG Bard character

goes downward

hit the note!

Or maybe hands on drums. The longer you can sustain it the more powerful attack. But it does things like be-comming faster.

2.) There is an Inn where you can buy a one time heal as always. But if you pay a lot extra you can buy an HP or MP key, or both. Beside the inn there are two key holes, one releases the HP orb you grab, to restore health, the other for MP. After you buy the key you can use it as often as you want.

MP HP ~ INN

3.) Magic crystals give you power over things of the same color (If a dragon is mostly green then use the green crystal, for example.)

AJC

USE of THis Book

This is a public domain book. The idea of it is to provide free new ideas. It is my contribution to the game making community.

Feel free to use it in whatever way, with or without credit, and to share it, or if you want, sell it. It is not held to personal rights over it — it is a public domain book.

I cannot entirely guarantee that the ideas here have not been done before. From what I know they have not been.

& thank you for reading my book.

- Adam Jeremy Capps.

Also Enjoy These Books By Adam Jeremy Capps:

The New Video Game Idea Book
The New Game Makers Bible
Making A Great Video Game
New Video Game Ideas